BASKETBALL

BY VALERIE BODDEN

Published by Creative Education and Creative Paperbacks
P.O. Box 227, Mankato, Minnesota 56002
Creative Education and Creative Paperbacks
are imprints of The Creative Company
www.thecreativecompany.us

Design and production by The Design Lab
Art direction by Rita Marshall
Printed in the United States of America

Photographs by Dreamstime (Dave Bredeson, Christinlola),
iStockphoto (t_kimura), Shutterstock (Albo, Aaron Amat,
Aleksandar Grozdanovski, Mark Herreid, JoffreyM, Mr
Doomits, Eugene Onischenko, ostill, Mark Prytherch,
Torsak Thammachote), Thinkstock (Big Cheese Photo)

Library of Congress Cataloging-in-Publication Data
Bodden, Valerie.
Basketball / Valerie Bodden.
p. cm. — (Making the play)
Includes index.
Summary: An elementary introduction to the physics involved in the
sport of basketball, including scientific concepts such as launch
angles and inertia, and actions such as dribbling and shooting.
ISBN 978-1-60818-654-9 (hardcover)
ISBN 978-1-62832-233-0 (pbk)
ISBN 978-1-56660-685-1 (eBook)
1. Basketball—Juvenile literature. 2. Physics—Juvenile literature. I. Title.

GV885.1.B64 2016
796.323—dc23   2015007570

CCSS: RI.1.1, 2, 3, 4, 5, 6, 7; RI.2.1, 2, 3, 5, 6, 7,
10; RI.3.1, 3, 5, 7, 8; RF.2.3, 4; RF.3.3

First Edition HC 9 8 7 6 5 4 3 2 1
First Edition PBK 9 8 7 6 5 4 3 2 1

CONTENTS

BASKETBALL AND SCIENCE

You dribble down the court. You get closer to the basket. You stop and toss the ball into the hoop. Two points!

6

Do you think about science when you play basketball? Probably not. But you use science anyway. A science called physics (*FIZ-icks*) can help you shoot, dribble, and pass. Let's see how!

LAUNCHING FORCE

You don't throw a basketball straight at the basket. If you did, it would bounce off. You have to push the ball above the basket. You throw it forward at the same time.

LAUNCH ANGLE

How much the ball goes up as it moves forward

A player close to the basket has to throw higher. It is different when you are farther away. You do not need as much upward **force**.

12

Think of a hose spraying water high in the air. The spray does not reach far.

STEADY SPEED

A ball keeps going where you threw it until something stops it. This is called inertia (*ih-NUR-shuh*).

INERTIA

An object stays still or moves at the same speed in a straight line until a force acts on it.

When you move at a **constant** speed,

inertia keeps the ball at your side.

You bounce the ball straight down.

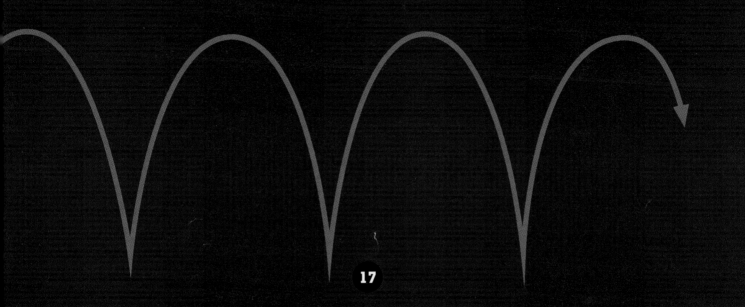

When you speed up, you need to push the ball in front of you. Otherwise, you'll leave it behind. How else can you use inertia in basketball? What about when you shoot a layup? Give it a try, and make the play!

INERTIA ON THE MOVE

If you drop something, it keeps moving at the same speed because of inertia.

WHAT YOU NEED

- Sidewalk chalk
- Frisbee

Mark an X on the sidewalk with chalk. This is your target. Back up about 30 feet (9.1 m) from the target. Then run toward it. Try to drop the Frisbee on the X as you run past. Did you hit the target? Try a few more times. When do you need to let go of the Frisbee to hit the target? Why do you think this is? What happens if you go faster or slower?

GLOSSARY

GLOSSARY

constant-staying the same, not changing

force-a push or a pull

READ MORE

Gifford, Clive. *Basketball*. Mankato, Minn.: Sea-to-Sea, 2010.

Gore, Bryson. *Physics*. Mankato, Minn.: Stargazer, 2009.

Walton, Ruth. *Let's Go to the Playground*.
Mankato, Minn.: Sea-to-Sea, 2013.

WEBSITES

DragonflyTV: Basketball
http://pbskids.org/dragonflytv
/show/basketball.html
Learn more about how your
launch angle can affect your shot.

StudyJams! Newton's
First Law: Inertia
http://studyjams.scholastic.com
/studyjams/jams/science/forces
-and-motion/inertia.htm
Watch a video about how inertia
keeps things moving.

INDEX

INDEX